NEWCASTLE/BLOODAXE POETRY SERIES: 15

GWYNETH LEWIS:
QUANTUM POETICS

NEWCASTLE/BLOODAXE POETRY SERIES

NEWCASTLE/BLOODAXE POETRY SERIES: 15

GWYNETH LEWIS

Quantum Poetics

NEWCASTLE / BLOODAXE POETRY LECTURES

BLOODAXE BOOKS

ISBN: 978 1 78037 070 5

First published 2015 by
Newcastle Centre for the Literary Arts,
Newcastle University,
Newcastle upon Tyne NE1 7RU,
in association with
Bloodaxe Books Ltd,
Eastburn,
South Park,
Hexham,
Northumberland NE46 1BS.

www.bloodaxebooks.com
For further information about Bloodaxe titles
please visit our website or write to
the above address for a catalogue.

Supported using public funding by
**ARTS COUNCIL
ENGLAND**

Cover design: Neil Astley & Pamela Robertson-Pearce.

Printed in Great Britain by Bell & Bain Limited, Glasgow, Scotland, on
acid-free paper sourced from mills with FSC chain of custody certification.

Contents

Acknowledgements

I would like to thank Newcastle Centre for the Literary Arts and Bloodaxe Books for the opportunity to give these lectures, which were delivered in March 2014. I'd like to thank Sean O'Brien, Bill Herbert, Linda Anderson, Gerry Wardle and Melanie Birch for their kind welcome and company during this period.

A version of the second lecture was delivered at the third British and Irish Contemporary Poetry Conference at Manchester, 12-14 September 2013. I'd like to thank Paul Batchelor for his close reading of that lecture. Richard Greene was a kind first reader of all three lectures.

I'd also like to thank Neil Astley for his long-term support.

The Stronger Life

I've called this series of lectures 'Quantum Poetics' because I'd like to argue that particle physics offers us several new ways of understanding poetry. I'm not talking here about science as a subject for poems, or about science as an analogy for how poetry works. In order to understand poetry, which is a material activity, we need to grasp some of the paradoxes of particle science. Poetry *is* a form of science. The poet uses herself as an experiment; she's both the observing mind and the sizzling substance in the test tube. This double existence – as subject and object – is what makes poetry ontologically significant. I don't accept the myth that science is any less imaginative than the arts, despite the fiction of "scientific objectivity" insisted on by some. I do, however, believe in facts and evidence, but see them as only one aspect of what, as humans, we can know about ourselves and the world.

It's a commonplace these days to regard art as therapeutic. My first lecture will examine this premise. A few years ago, I wrote a memoir about mental illness, *Sunbathing in the Rain: A Cheerful Book about Depression*. People are fond of linking creativity with madness. Being a zombie for months in the grip of depressive debility feels uncreative, but my experience is that it's a highly promising, if uncomfortable, state for the person undergoing it. Some civilians – those who haven't been conscripted into this particular forced march – seem to think that depression gives a writer that desperation that guarantees, if not quality, at least a certain artistic passion. They're wrong. Depression is, simply, a life-threatening disease like a narrowing of the arteries. However, this reaction does tell us a lot about what we think health is and what we wish writing were.

My second lecture will ask: where do poets live? to which nation to they belong? I was brought up speaking Welsh. I've

9

been bilingual from an early age and have chosen to continue to write in Welsh because, for a poet to throw away her first linguistic love seems to me perverse. Not that I'm against second or even third affairs. When writers listen to language, they're attentive, not to only words, but to the music on which those words are strung like beads. A writer doesn't have to be multilingual to understand the field that exists between languages. These deep structures of meaning are poetry's terrain and can't be described in terms of nationality. I'm going to suggest some ways in which quantum physics can help us to identify and explore that place which is, among other things, the very source of artistic health.

In the third lecture, I'll consider poetic form in relation to quantum physics, suggesting that there's a deep congruence between the structure of the physical world and poetry as an art. In certain ways, the world behaves like a poem and poetry itself is a kind of science. The accuracy of what poets say is just as important as the scrupulosity of experimental observation in scientific research.

Together these lectures explore how quantum entanglement and probability give us the conception of poetry as a universe or, more properly, multiple worlds. This first is light on physics but I hope, by the end of the third, that my argument will have convinced you that mental health, musicality and poetic form can all be described in terms consistent with quantum physics – and that they're all aspects of the same issue.

*

Mental health and its relationship to writing are subjects that have preoccupied me for a long time. I grew up in a household dominated by my mother's depression. When I left, I found, to my dismay, that I also suffered from the disease. In my late thirties, when I'd been working as a television producer at the BBC for a number of years, I suffered the worst episode so far. During that time I looked for an encouraging book to read and found that all the publications available were... depressing. So, as I recovered, and before I'd forgotten the extreme existential horror of severe depression, I decided to note some ways I'd learned of coping with it. I wrote *Sunbathing in the Rain: A Cheerful Book about Depression* in short paragraphs, for those who'd lost their ability to concentrate. Through trial and error, I'd learned some basic principles about what not to do when you're depressed:

> Don't attempt the Bible, *War and Peace*, or *À la Recherche du Temps Perdu* [...]
> Don't join a gym for the first time in fifteen years[...]
> Don't make any decisions while you're depressed [such as:]
> Running away to Brazil
> Going blonde (scuppered by my hairdresser, who refused to do it without a doctor's note confirming that I was of sound mind).
> Training as a radio operator on board a Scandinavian tanker and going to sea [...]
> Taking the veil [...]
> There will be plenty of time to become a nun when you're feeling more cheerful.[1]

The book was also an artistic autobiography. For as long as I can remember, being able to write and publish has been at the centre of my well being. Over ten years of psychotherapy had shown me that, rather than being a random chemical event in my blood, my depression is always linked to my refusing, in some way, to do my work as a poet. Far from being the result of writing too much, depression always happens to me when I'm writing too little or writing too much of the wrong kind of thing.

Not everyone in your life wants you to be a writer. It takes a good deal of self-confidence and generosity on the part of a loved one to give you the freedom and imaginative space that being a poet requires. But, if it's in you, poetry's no pussycat either:

> Poetry has acquired a fluffy image, which is totally at odds with its real nature. It's not pastel colours, but blood-red and black. If you don't obey it was a force in your life, it will tear you to pieces [...]

> Unwritten poems are a force to be feared [...] Killing the source of poetry in you is an offence against the gods because it shows contempt for the strongest force of truth in your life. It's like killing the best part of yourself. It's an act that requires penance and the perpetrator isn't easily absolved.[2]

If the price of not writing is high, it appears that writing poetry carries its own cost. William Blake kept a print of Dürer's etching of *Melancholia* on the wall of his studio. Kay Redfield Jamison, in *Touched with Fire*, suggests that poets are forty times more likely to be manic-depressive than the rest of the population and eight times more likely to commit suicide.[3] Even though I suffer from depression, I don't feel like a delicate creature. I was delighted, therefore, to discover a 1998 paper that challenges the link between creativity and mental illness. The meta-analysis shows that, of twenty-nine studies, fifteen find no evidence to support a link, nine find a link and five have unclear conclusions.[4] Redfield Jamison's statistics begin to look like another version of a myth of the tortured artist.

Nevertheless, being a writer is far from being undemanding. I was once trying to explain to a ten-year-old relative that poetry is hard work. She and I had often written poems together. 'What do you mean?' she said, 'You just sit down and do it!' I tried to explain that it's one thing to write verses for family and quite another being productive when you really don't feel like it. What I wanted to say, but didn't, was that the real job goes something like this: it's a refusal to toe any party line, even that of your own ego; a willingness to explore the raw biographical material of your life, however volatile. You have to negotiate a way of telling your truth without offending your nearest and dearest so much that you end up in Coventry. You need an ability to leave your own body and enter into other imaginative worlds so thoroughly that you fear you'll never find a way back. It's to be open to the charge of wasting your time completely on playing with words. It's an activity in which you don't know what on earth you're doing, where nothing makes sense – sometimes for a long time – and when it does, inspiration comes not as a result of your own ingenuity, but due to another force – let's say the voice of the language – being in charge.

I've never seen it described better than in Regina Derieva's poem 'When you burn':

> When you burn
> your bridges behind you,
> it follows nothing
> is left.
> Even the road
> no longer knows you,
> as you stumble along it.
> Your eyes grow ashen,
> your mouth is like a well
> from which words no longer gush.
> You don't care
> whether they do or don't believe
> the fact that
> you are dead.[5]

Because the polarity of values is reversed, being dead (depressed or defeated) in this landscape is the best way to be alive. Here the unsuspected, the unthinkable, begin to come to light and act on the poet/patient, giving him or her a voice, new form. My great discovery about depression is that it isn't an enemy but an ally. Its meaninglessness is the poet's best friend, showing her where not to go. Then, form gives her clues: warmer, warm, hot, boiling!

The psychoanalyst Marion Milner's wonderful book *On Not Being Able to Paint* shows the hinterland that exists for all the arts. Milner explores the humiliating difference between an artist's intention and what she's able to produce on paper. This galling gap is what discourages perfectionists. Milner decided to sit with the issue, rather than letting it distract her from the process:

> what I found now was that, at times, if one could bring oneself to look at the gap, allow oneself to see both the ideal and the failure to live up to it in one moment of vision, and without the urge to interfere and alter oneself to fit the ideal, then the ideal and the fact seemed somehow to enter into relation and produce something quite new, something that had nothing to do with being pleased with oneself for having lived up to an ideal or miserable because of having failed to... For it was a watching part which, by being able to see the two opposing differences of standard, or ideal, and actuality, in relation to each other, was by this very act able to bring about an integration, a new way of being which somehow combined the essence of both.[6]

It has its pleasures but, I can tell you, the artistic life keeps you humble. An apocryphal Dylan Thomas saying describes the poet's vocation as walking on your eyeballs over broken glass. As this year is the centenary of his birth, I'd like to stay with Dylan Thomas for a moment. I once saw a vial filled with a yellowish fluid, purporting to be Dylan Thomas's sweat. It's now thought that Thomas didn't die – as usually thought – of alcoholic excess; his post mortem showed little evidence of cirrhosis of the liver.[7] On 16 November 1954 Elizabeth Bishop wrote that she and the critic Joseph Frank had been to lunch with Dylan Thomas. The occasion had disturbed her:

> I said to Joe later something trite about 'Why he'll kill himself if he goes on like this,' and Joe said promptly, 'Don't be silly. Can't you see a man like that doesn't *want* to live?' [...] But his poetry has that desperate win-or-lose-all quality, of course – and of course too it eliminates everything from life except something almost beyond human supportability after a while.[8]

Poets voluntarily submit themselves to a state of mind which most people – aside from monks – will avoid like the plague.

They develop artistic and emotional strategies which turn this apparently unpromising place into a highly rewarding landscape. I would argue that the poet's value to society primarily lies in his or her resilience in the face of dread, in their insistence on shaping something forceful, energetic and delightful out of this blankness. These artistic strategies are the very ones that can get one out of depression. Far from being the victim of depression, the poet is more like a member of the Special Forces who goes into enemy terrain to execute the most risky of existential manoeuvres. If he or she succumbs from time to time, it's not as a result of being over-sensitive but from spending far, far more time on the field of battle than does the ordinary soldier. This is one reason, I believe, Wallace Stevens asserted that 'the poet is the stronger life'.

Elizabeth Bishop tried to imagine what might 'cure' poets. In the same letter as quoted above, she said:

> Poets should have self-doubts left out of their systems completely – as one can see most of the surviving ones seem to have. But look at poor Cal – and Marianne, who hangs on just by the skin of her teeth and the most elaborate paranoia I've ever heard of.[9]

A self-doubt lobotomy might make poets more content but I distrust all speech which is too certain of its conclusions. Bishop concluded that 'Dylan made most of our contemporaries seem small and disgustingly self-seeking and cautious and hypocritical + cold.'[10] He also 'had an amazing gift for a kind of naked communication that makes a lot of poetry look like translation'.[11] We shall never know what Dylan Thomas would have achieved as a writer, if he'd survived his crisis in New York. However, it's clear that he was happiest when he was writing poems. In the last years of his life he completed very few, compared to his prodigious output when his life was more routine. In her memoir *Poets in their Youth* Eileen Simpson, who was married to John Berryman, wrote about a whole generation of poets decimated by mental illness and alcoholism. John Berryman was with Dylan Thomas when he died. In 1972 Berryman killed himself. Simpson concluded:

> Many – I, too, at moments – blamed the suicide on John's having
> been a poet. The litany of suicides among poets is long. After a
> while I began to feel that I'd missed the obvious. It was the
> poetry that had kept him alive. His father had committed suicide
> at forty. With as much reason and with a similar psychic make-
> up, John had been tempted more than once to follow his father's
> example. That he lived seventeen years longer than John Allyn
> Smith, that he died a 'veteran of life' was thanks to his gift.[12]

So, how does poetry keep a person alive? In her book on
graphomania, *The Midnight Demon*, neurologist Alice Flaherty
suggests that language itself may well be the first mood-altering
substance. Poetic metre has a biological effect on the body. The
dominant rhythm of English is iambic, with an unstressed
syllable followed by a stressed one. You can remember it by
saying to yourself, 'Iámbic says, "I ám, I ám".' This rhythm is
linked to the most basic sound of the human body, the heartbeat.
Experiments on rats show that rhythm produces the feel-good
dopamine as a reward in the brain. Dic Jones, Welsh farmer and
master poet said that he used to get his best ideas while he was
in the milking parlour – if you've never heard an automatic
milking machine, it's like having a heartbeat magnified so much
that you can hear the blood spurt inside the chambers of the
heart. Research conducted in Cardiff University suggests that
the rhythm created by an activity like knitting, requiring some
skill – but not too much – produces a meditative state that is
very beneficial to the depressed. Tiny eye movements required by
the craft are also being used in the treatment of Post Traumatic
Stress Disorder. A course of heroic couplets for low-grade
depression? Complex forms like the villanelle and sestina for
emergency cases? Hardly. I'm certainly not suggesting that
poets who don't write in metre and rhyme are risking their
health. Free verse is the most demanding form of all.
Anecdotally, one thinks of Ted Hughes believing that writing
too much prose, rather than poetry, had contributed to his own
illness. There is, however, a credible argument to be made for

the rigours of poetry being part of our collective resistance to linguistic anomie.

The poet is the unseen first and final draft of a poem. The poet doesn't know how to exist without undergoing change by means of successive poems. Words left on the paper are the byproduct of the main event, which is this transformation. The poem's body alters that of its inventor. Depression can act in the same way; if I survive an episode, I come out of it knowing more. Whatever I'm required to do to live through the poem/depression offers the best answer for my health. I refuse, therefore, to see depression as an aberrant state outside the creative cycle. By this, I categorically don't mean that you have to be depressed to write a poem – in fact, the healthier and happier one is, the better, even if you want to write a tragedy.

There's a tenth-century Welsh myth about Taliesin, the archetypal poet, which catches this nicely. The legend's very elaborate, and I'm going to come back to it later but, suffice it to say here that there's a witch, a magic potion and a servant involved. Ceridwen, a wise woman, employs a servant, Gwion to stir a cauldron brewing a drink that endows wisdom; she intends to give this to her son. At the crucial moment, Gwion imbibes the drops of poetic inspiration. When she wakes up, Ceridwen is furious. In terror, Gwion turns himself into a hare, but Ceridwen changes into a greyhound to hunt him; Gwion disguises himself as an ear of corn, Ceridwen, transforms herself into a hen, eats him and then gives birth to him. The only way to be safe is to assent to contintual metamorphosis. In the end, Gwion is cast out to sea in a skin, a symbolic womb, for forty years, and turns into the poet Taliesin. The sea will be an important part of my next lecture, but I just want to note here that the wily boy doesn't become a poet until he submits himself to oceanic forces.

Writing about how he developed his poetic language, W.B. Yeats draws a distinction between words as units and as a process which the poet undergoes, like a voyage:

It was a long time before I had made a language to my liking; I began to make it when I discovered some twenty years ago that I must seek, not as Wordsworth thought, words in common use, but a powerful and passionate syntax.[13]

Here, the adjective 'passionate' means much more than 'strong felt'. Yeats evokes the shadow religious meaning of the passion, with its suggestion not only of undergoing a painful experience but also of consenting to it. It implies a conscious decision to allow an experience to shape you. Taliesin becomes a fish, not only to escape from his pursuer, but to know what it's like to breathe underwater and to be subject to the tides.

One of the huge benefits of spending time in the liminal territory of not knowing what to say in a poem is that it makes you fearless about challenging all received ideas. This is why Joseph Brodsky described poetry as the business end of evolution, which is life spontaneously improving on its imagination of itself. Wallace Stevens is very precise about how poets do this: 'the imagination is the power that enables us to perceive the normal in the abnormal, the opposite of chaos in chaos. It does this every day in arts and letters.'[14] In the poem's disorder, all categories are under artistic pressure, so that the writer may come up with startling new ways of looking at old questions For example, in 'Eleven Addresses to the Lord', John Berryman perceived illness not as a failure but as reward:

Make too me acceptable at the end of time
in my degree, which then Thou wilt award.
Cancer, senility, mania,
I pray I may be ready with my witness.[15]

We're accustomed to thinking of illness as a punishment rather than an honour. These lines force us to imagine an order of values in which sickness is good because it's one more opportunity to serve God. It's a vision of heaven.

While this kind of startling category change may sound psychically frightening, and it can be, there are ways in which the art of poetry can earth this lightning bolt and make it safe.

Although they may be slogging away in a solitary corner, writers are never alone when they're working in the communal medium, language. Part of learning to be a poet is knowing how to keep good company. This doesn't just mean poets who are still alive, but falling in love with, reading and memorising the work of poets long dead and incorporating that into your own work. A few years ago I wrote an epic called *A Hospital Odyssey*. I would no more go it alone on a big project like this than I'd set off on a voyage without VHF radio and a first aid kit. Dante had Virgil, so, in *A Hospital Odyssey* I decided to follow the model of François Villon, the fifteenth-century French poet whose work will be familiar to you in the refrain 'Mais où sont les neiges d'antan?' 'Where is the drift of last year's snow?' [16] I admired Villon's colloquial directness and ability to laugh at human folly without bitterness. He writes about human flesh with gusto and without shame. I needed to borrow Villon's poetic body. From his *ballade* form, I adapted a five-line stanza which suited the pace of my own breath, took it for a test drive and absconded with the vehicle.

No epic poem can get under way without a proper invocation to the gods. I couldn't call on Zeus with any conviction, so I decided to invoke the spirit of language through the poets I admire. Preparing to write a long poem is a period of intense anxiety. I needed all the help I could get.:

I've said already that I won't feel well
till this poem's finished and I find what I mean
about health and loving. It's a hospital,
this place I'm constructing line by line,
with clinics in it and sunlit rooms

open to anyone. Words are my health,
the struggle to hear and transcribe the tune
behind what I'm given by word of mouth,
it's the only work that can make me immune
to lying. May my language gene

grant me haemoglobin and many platelets,
potency deep inside bone marrow.

My safety lies with other poets
who've shown the way they took through shadows.
Milton, Villon, be with me now.

I want to capture what it is to care
for someone you love who's very ill,
how quickly you age as you see them suffer,
you'd do anything to make them well,
but you can't. Now help me, Virgil,

give me the strength of your long sinews
to capture that terrible smile
couples exchange when they both know
the score. Help me to draw on wells
that are clean and kind and plentiful.

What do you say when someone you love
is dying and there's nothing you can do
to stop it happening, and you're alive
and well, and nowhere near through
adoring them, and you can't follow?

One body's never enough. My reach
is long. Of one thing you can be sure
I'll never give up on this endless search,
for you and it's my only cure,
to touch you. Yes, stranger, I mean you.[17]

If poetry can be a health-giving activity, it's only logical that
it can also have injurious effects. Music that's sweet to me
might set your teeth on edge. Think of the classical music used
to soothe elderly patients but to drive gangs of teenagers from
market town centres. It's claimed that some primal rage
therapy, can, rather than proving cathartic, simply amplify the
anger a person feels. I've had this happen to me with poems
that I should not have written – either because they were self-
indulgent, spiteful or simply not true enough to pass muster.
Instead of making me feel better they made me feel worse. In
the Taliesin myth, Gwion, who profited hugely from the
muses' gifts, also reminds us of this toxicity. According to Eric
P. Hamp, Gwion's name means 'the Little Prototypic Poison'.

By drinking the brew, Gwion himself becomes, in some way, a concentrate of that poison. Poets have never been easy companions or tranquil citizens.

A few years ago, I thought that I'd encountered an example of a poet to whom I was allergic. It's said that small doses of toxins aren't harmful to the body, but have a useful role in stimulating the immune system. W.H. Auden admired the rhythms of Laura Riding's work. I set out to read her 1938 collection of poems, re-edited and published by Carcanet. My reaction was strong. Finally! A poet whose work I couldn't stand. Riding was a scandal in her time, not only as one of Robert Graves's 'muses', but also because, after gaining a reputation as a poet in her own right, she gave up writing altogether. I recently returned to her Collected in order to see what had so riled me about Riding's work. The pencil marks in the book showed I'd paid very close attention to the poems. The annotations highlight many striking passages, such as this from 'Respect for the Dead':

Does the truth then live?
No, the truth does not die.
The truth and the dead do not die.
Respect the truth and the dead.

The truth is the one person alive.
It goes for a walk every evening
After day and before night.
It goes for a walk with the dead.[18]

There is something compelling about the remorseless logic of these end-stopped lines, combined with the one run-on line, which enacts the wider perspective that going for a walk gives. Looking back, over my notes, I see a succession of poems that have influenced my work in the last twenty years. So, a little poetic toxin can act as a fertile irritant and may be a very good thing for a writer.

Dylan Thomas's career has been used to make him the poster boy of the drunken, chaotic poet. Even in his centenary year, the myth of Dylan Thomas as a 'druid of the broken body' is more potent than his reputation as a serious avant-garde writer. It's still difficult to get people to read his poetry seriously. I would argue that his personal difficulties came not from his tumultuous life but from aesthetic choices made in his poems. Before his death, Thomas was planning to write a long poem in the character of Taliesin. He was to be

> the godhead, the author, the first cause, architect, lamp-lighter, the beginning word, the anthropomorphic bawler-out and black-baller, the quintessence, scapegoat, martyr, maker
> – He, on top of a hill in Heaven.[19]

Thomas's Taliesin is more than a shape-shifter, he is God himself – always a dangerous persona for a mortal to adopt.

At other times, Thomas appears to regard language as a divinity:

> such sand-storms and ice-blasts of words, such slashing of humbug, and humbug too, such staggering peace, such enormous laughter, such and so many blinding bright lights breaking across the just-awaking wits and splashing all over the pages in a million bits and pieces all of which were words, words, words, and each of which was alive forever in its own delight and glory and oddity and light.[20]

The shadows of Taliesin and Ceridwen in their desperate chase flit through this passage.

In 'The Colour of Saying', Thomas describes his early, simple, relationship with words:

> Once it was the colour of saying
> Soaked my table the uglier side of a hill
> With a capsized field where a school sat still
> And a black and white patch of girls playing.[21]

Elsewhere, words are scarecrows – not the aim of a search, but merely symbols to distract scavengers from the real goal of the poet, the crop around the figure. Thomas continues that, having gown up, his work is to dismantle that vision of language as innocent: 'The gentle seaslides of saying I must undo / That all the charmingly drowned arise to cockcrow and kill.' He's saying here that the poet can raise the dead. The end of the poem has no illusion about the cost of this project to the poet: 'Now my saying shall be my undoing.' This is the moment, I believe, where we see Dylan Thomas box himself into the contradiction that led to his later troubles. As with all writers, his life followed his writing, not the other way around. This position was far more harmful to him than his exploits with whisky.

To end this first lecture, I want speculate that there is an even more basic way that poetry contributes to the health of the poet – and, by extension, his or her readers. Those of you who are interested in science will know that the Nobel Prize last year was awarded to Peter Higgs, who theorised that a boson – an infinitessimally small particle that had never been seen – is what gives objects their mass. His hypothesis was proved by an experiment in the CERN's Large Hadron Collider where scientists saw the signature of the particle. Until then, mass had been a mystery and scientists were at a loss to explain what caused inertia and made matter behave as though it were immersed in a sea of treacle. I want now to strip poetry down to its basic particles and speculate about the properties of its Higgs field. Chinese poet Yang Wanli (1127-1206) has described this terrain beautifully:

> Now what is poetry? If you say it is simply a matter of words, I will say 'A good poet gets rid of words.' If you say it is simply a matter of meaning, I will say, 'A good poet gets rid of meaning,' But, you say, if words and meaning are dispensed with, where is the poetry? To this, I reply, 'Get rid of words and meaning, and there is still poetry.' [22]

This is the rhythm that is located behind words and metre, in the deep structure of the art. It's a quantum field of potential. That's the place I will discuss in my next lecture.

What Country, Friends, Is This?

In the second scene of *Twelfth Night*, Shakespeare's cross-dressing heroine, Viola, enters the play in the company of sailors:

> VIOLA
> What country, friends, is this?
> CAPTAIN
>   This is Illyria, lady.
> VIOLA
> And what should I do in Illyria?
>   (*l.* 1f)[1]

Our introduction to Illyria is musical. Duke Orsino's famous speech 'If music be the food of love, play on, / Give me excess of it' responds to harmony. The therapeutic effect of melody doesn't last long, however, and the Duke becomes irritated:

>   Enough, no more;
> 'Tis not so sweet now as it was before.
> O spirit of love, how quick and fresh art thou
> That, notwithstanding thy capacity
> Receiveth as the sea, nought enters there,
> Of what validity and pitch soe'er,
> But falls into abatement and low price
> Even in a minute. So full of shapes is fancy
> That it alone is high fantastical.
>   (*l.* 7f)[2]

The dominant image is love as the sea. The music which, a second ago soothed the Duke's frustration in love, is described in financial terms, and suffers a catastrophic reduction in value

– 'abatement' and 'low price'. With his short attention span, Orsino doesn't investigate the logical idea that, in such a rhythmic medium, jetsam might just as quickly rise as fall in value, if he had stayed to listen. Even so, it's from this sea that Viola and the plot of the play emerge in the next scene.

Shakespeare's Illyria, probably refers to the area which is now Albania, the kingdom ruled over by Cadmus and Harmony – note the musical association. According to T.W. Craik, Shakespeare was here remembering a passage from Ovid's *Metamorphoses*. Cadmus and Harmony are shipwrecked on the coast of 'Illirie'. Another source for *Twelfth Night* was *Riche His Farewell to Militarie Profession*, published in 1581. Written by Barnabe Riche, a former sea captain, the novel shows a woman, Silla, deciding to follow her beloved Apolonius from her home in Crete to Constantinople. She dresses up as a low-born woman in order to be safe. However, the captain of the vessel she boards decides to rape her but, mercifully, Silla's virtue is saved by a providential storm, the ancestor of a similar blow in *The Tempest*. This turbulent weather is another way of describing the internal landscape inhabited by poets. It's inhospitable but potentially very productive:

> this storme continued all that daie and the next night, and thei beeyng driuen to put romer before the winde to keepe the Gallie ahed the Billowe, were driuen vppon the maine shore, where the Gallie brake all to peeces [...] Silla her self beying in the Caben as you haue heard, tooke holde of a Cheste that was the Captaines, the whiche by the onely prouidence of GOD brought her safe to the shore, the whiche when she had recouered [....] she brake open the Chest that brought her to lande, wherin she found good store of coine, and sondrie sutes of apparell. (*ll.* 236-70)[3]

The turbulence allows Silla to take the captain's chattels, giving her financial power and the wardrobe with which she can cross-dress at will. She becomes captain of her own fate. The storm is the muse of Riche's novel, it's generative, it travels into and inspires Shakespeare's play. It's the ancestor of the tempest in Shakespeare's last play of that name.

In my first lecture, I described how poets spend a lot of time in a seemingly unrewarding terrain avoided by most people. Their familiarity with it gives them an uncommon existential stamina, equipping them with the same skills needed to counter depression. It's the Sahara when you're doing an ultra-marathon and can't remember what on earth possessed you to undertake such a task. I argued that, in engaging with such a place of not knowing, the poet allows it to shape not only individual poems but also, more importantly, the self. In this lecture, I want to identify and describe another aspect of that same place. This time it's watery, rather than dry, but it's a desert nevertheless. It can, I believe, be identified in most poets' work. It is a quantum centre – note, not *the* centre – and it behaves in a spectacularly unexpected manner.

Twentieth-century physics demonstrated that, at the quantum level, matter and time behave in counterintuitive ways. Experiments in the last couple of decades have proved that a test conducted on a particle in one place affects matter in a totally different one.[4] This is known as quantum entanglement. Scientists such as David Bohm have argued that, however distant phenomena are from each other, they are connected:

> The very facts of science [...] the actual data (from physics to physiology) seemed to make sense only if we assume some sort of implicit or unifying or transcendental ground underlying the explicit data.[5]

That is, no matter how many trillions of miles of space separates two particles, from the point of view of entanglement, they are in exactly the same spot. Einstein contended that there is no such thing as absolute and universal time but Bohm posits a field underlying the visible world. Bohm uses the two terms 'explicate' – unfolded – and 'implicate' – folded – in order to distinguish between the two. So, within separate things and events, there is an enfolded realm of wholeness. In Ken Wilber's words:

What appears to be a stable, tangible, visible, audible world, said Bohm, is an illusion. It is dynamic and kaleidoscopic – not really "there". What we normally see is the explicit, or unfolded, order of things, rather like watching a movie. But there is an underlying order that is mother and father to this second-generation reality.[6]

If this is true at a quantum level, even thought we're not physically aware of it at the huge human scale, then this reality must have effects on how our brains and, therefore, art, work. Bohm's conclusion is that 'it is possible to have an implicate order with regard to time as well as to space [...] to say that in any given period of time the whole of time may be enfolded'.[7]

Bohm argues that reality is a hologram – that is, an entity, any part of which contains the whole. I came across a book about this holographic paradigm by chance just after I'd graduated and it's shaped how I understand both literature and the physical universe. It means, basically, that I've stopped believing in any one place being privileged over any another as a centre. This has, of course, a political dimension, but not along party lines. I'm anti-centrist but not nationalist. Perhaps I'm a Christian anarchist. To me, the most exciting part of writing an epic, *A Hospital Odyssey*, was that it made me pay attention to the cosmology by which I operate. I found an astronomer at a party and asked if he'd teach me some particle physics. He happened to be looking for a poet to write a poem for his department website, so that worked out well. Maris, my main character – we're at sea again – is in the Underworld, in search of stem cells for her sick husband. My island is Hy-Brazil, a floating piece of land from Celtic mythology. Maris has met Aneurin Bevan, founder of the National Health Service and he acts as a guide for a while. She asks:

'What *is* this place?' Bevan was silent
a second. 'This isn't solid ground
but a place of potential, actions that resound

forward through time and, sometimes, echo
back to affect events. This island floats

through space and time. Here we foreknow
the future's genome. It's like a boat
riding the waves of an implicate

ocean behind the things we see.
Things can happen and unhappen at once,
then happen again. Probability
waves break on our beaches, the first surge destroys,
the second restores. Nobody knows

how such flux happens. Uncertainty
is this island's principle. Each cove
both exists and doesn't. The geography
is everything possible, because love
believes in it all.'[8]

I'm sure that being bilingual in Welsh and English from an early age weaned me from the idea of a linguistic centre. Twenty percent of the Welsh population have the language. This gives a false impression of what it is to be part of a linguistic minority: you don't *feel* like anything but a complete society. We spoke Welsh at home, but my father taught me English at twenty-seven months. In Cardiff, growing up, I hardly ever used my English. I spoke English only with friends on the street, in Brownies and ballet lessons. I was educated in Welsh to 'A'-level, went to youth club, chapel – all in Welsh. When I went to England for an university admissions interview, my father and I practised my English all the way up to college – a strange, stilted conversation. We reverted to Welsh with relief on the way back. I count in English but dream in both languages but mainly in images. When I'm in deep trouble, I pray and swear in Welsh and I want Welsh-language psalms read to me on my deathbed.

For a small country of three million people, Wales is riven by complex cultural allegiances. The English and Welsh-language traditions in Wales have distinct characters. In the 1970s, Welsh nationalism was aggressive, even towards some Welsh speakers. I remember being told during a drunken evening in North Wales that I wasn't even Welsh because Cardiff wasn't in the heartland and didn't count. *Never* assume that members of any minority are cosy in that community. I had a double whammy of alienation. At Cambridge, the idea of being a Welsh-language poet was regarded a something preposterous, as uncool as Morris dancing and far more subversive. I fled to America to find neutral ground and sort out where my allegiances lay – to language, society or to poetry itself.

In the end, I decided to live in a ménage à trois and to write in both Welsh and English. The Welsh is like the older wife who thinks things should be done strictly according to tradition. The English is the younger recruit – energetic, seductive, eager for experience. Treated in the right way, of course, the senior wife has a sense of humour and wears moon boots under her skirts. The bride, for all her modernity, knows how to veil herself and pray to the old gods.

In me, the two languages constitute an underground water system. They burst out of the earth in two different streams but are of the same nature. Writing in Welsh changes what I can do in English and vice the versa. Both languages seem to be going on inside me simultaneously whenever I'm writing in one or the other. I sometimes deliberately play the one off the other. In his memoir of Istanbul, Orhan Pamuk concludes that 'Istanbul's greatest virtue is its people's ability to see the city through both Western and Eastern eyes'.[9] Any cultural position involving divided loyalties is personally painful but it does give you the ability to see more than one side of an argument. It also innoculates you against national ra-raism and gives one very sensitive antennae for the detection of territorialism. One recent example. Matthew Hollis's immensely readable *Now All Roads Lead to France: the Last Years of Edward Thomas* (2011)[10] portrays an exclusively English Thomas. Yet, both Thomas's parents were Welsh and the poet wrote in a notebook of 1899 that 'Wales indeed is my soul's native land, if the soul can be said to have a *patria* – or rather, a *matria*'.[11] The point here is not to make a counter-claim for Thomas as an exclusively Welsh poet – that would be reproducing the same erroneous model – but to say that mono-culturalism does the richness of his work a disservice. Nationhood is a lazy category by which to denote writers but it is something with which to begin. At a recent Venice Biennale, artist Ai Weiwei was chosen to represent Germany in the French Pavilion as a Chinese citizen. He commented:

> As new technological and scientific developments challenge our way of thinking, the condition we live in and our modes of expression, artists should always be the first to become aware of the change that arises and the boundaries that it destroys.[12]

It's no accident that I think of my two languages and their relationship to each other in terms of water. Irish-language poet Nuala Ní Dhomhnaill has used the legend of the amphibious mermen and women to describe bilingualism. The mermaid who comes ashore – that is, who learns to speak English – is in a very uncomfortable position:

> Níl sí anseo nó ansúd.
> Ní hiasc is ní feoil í.
> Uaireanta searann sí polliáirí a sróine
> i slí is go dtuigfeá go b'ann a bhíonn sí
> a bá san aer
> faoi mar a bheadh breac go mbeirfeá air le slat
> is go leagfá aniar ar an bport é.
>
> She's neither here nor there.
> She's neither fish nor flesh.
> Sometimes she has a sharp intake of breath through her nostrils
> that would make you think she's
> drowning in air,
> like a trout you'd caught with a rod
> and taken to the bank.[13]

That this sea exists in the mind is even more clear in a poem on 'The Assimilated Merfolk':

> Fágann na rabhartaí earraigh a rianta fós
> ar chlathacha cosanta a n-aigne; gach tonnchosc díobh
> ina ghlib ag bruth farraige is ag brúscar raice –
> focail a scuabtar isteach mar a bheadh carbháin charraige

ar líne bharra taoide nuair a bhuaileann an ré roithleacáin
aimsir ré an tSathairn, focail a thugann scáil
na seanré fós leo, focail ar nós
'más reamhar, com seang, meanmain uallaigh'.

The high spring tides leave their mark
on the sea-walls of their minds, the edge of every breaking wave
ragged with flotsam and jetsam and other wreckage,
words carried ashore like the shells of sea-urchins
and left at the high-water mark when they get the head-staggers
at the time of the Saturday moon, words that are still imbued
with the old order of things, phrases like
'wide-thighs, narrow-waist, hare-brain'.[14]

What's important here is that the energy for these movements of mind don't come from words themselves, but from the waves and tides – much larger rhythms. Words are carried by these but don't create them. This is why, in translation, the words are the last thing you deal with – you have to catch the tune underneath them first.

The only person I've seen to describe this source of the rhythms on which words ride is the Catholic theologian Jacques Maritain. In his Mellon Lectures of 1953, Maritain gave an account of the artistic impulse in the unconscious as essentially musical. If you picture the unconscious as a musical sea, then Maritain christened the waves behind the artistic rhythm 'pulsions', a cross, perhaps between 'rhythms' and 'impulses.' I wish he'd found a better word, but he's identifying something essential to poetry. What he means is *'meaning* set free in a *motion*: that is to say, a kind of melody'.[15] This is 'emotion as form' and it 'carries within itself infinitely more than itself'.[16] The part of the mind Maritain is describing is 'a musical unconscious for, being one with the root activity of reason, it contains from the start a germ of melody'.[17]

This, I believe, is the place which all artists know and which I'm calling Illyria. It's not geographical but internal. It's pre-verbal and pre-lyrical. It's a wet place and is described, I think, explicitly in many poets' work. Here's Sean O'Brien, a very watery poet, describing 'The Mere':

> Its poplars and willows and sludge. Its gnat-clouds.
> Smell of cooking animal at dusk. Grey-greeness.
> Soup-suspension. Its having been
> Here all along. It is nowhere, serves nothing, lives
> On your behalf when you are absent.
> Now they want to drain it.[18]

Of course, the authorities want to drain this mere: it's anathema to power. Much has been made of Thomas Hardy's burst of writing on the death of his first wife. Whatever we make of it in biographical terms, the poem 'The Voice', suggests to me that one of the reasons for this rush of poems is that thinking of his dead wife gave him exactly the right focal distance to approach his Illyria. The poet describes how he hears his wife calling to him and asks:

> Or is it only the breeze, in its listlessness
> Travelling across the wet mead to me here,
> You being ever dissolved to existlessness,
> Heard no more again far or near? [19]

Am I being over-obsessed with the dampness of Illyria when I notice that the field over which the wind or voice comes is 'wet?'

It's often forgotten that R.S. Thomas was the son of a captain. Many of his poems are seascapes. Take this, for example, called 'The Sea':

>   A child's
> Plaything? It has hard whips
> That it cracks, and knuckles
> To pummel you. It scrubs
> And scours; it chews rocks
> To sand; its embraces
> Leave you without breath. Mostly
> It is a stomach, where bones,
> Wrecks, continents are digested.[20]

This is more hostile than O'Brien's mere, and the sea's acidic juices remind me of Jonah in the whale or, more disturbingly, of Saturn, the god of melancholy, digesting his own children in his belly.

If I'm going to start judging poets by their moisture content, I'd have to call W.N. Herbert a vermouth of a writer – he's a dry watery poet. Herbert's *Omnesia*, is an attempt to describe the contemporary phenomenon of having access to more information than ever before but forgetting a larger proportion of it. This isn't unlike the half-forgotten, half-recalled knowledge in the subconscious which is the Illyrian mode. In Herbert's 'Looking Glass Falls' the water is frozen into a 'translucent pigtail' but it's still another state of water.[21] It's no accident that Herbert writes his indeterminate territory in Scots and with dizzying changes of register. 'Dichtung (Till Awa Wi It)' plays on the idea of the poem as a no-place:

> Thi message isnae information
> thi wey a train is no thi station
>   an a journey's no thi rail;
> thi message huz nae destination
> thi wey a voice is no narration
>   and yir life is no a tale.
> Thi message is an eisenin
>   that cell speak unto cell;
> that seabirds sing horizonin,
>   that deean men maun tell.
>   Thi message is aa presages
>   o whit we waant tae mean,
>   thi poem a golem
>   that canna speak, jist dream.[22]

Illyria and the island in *The Tempest* form part of Shakespeare's self-portrait as an artist. Theatr Genedlaethol Cymru, the Welsh-language National Theatre of Wales, commissioned me to translate *The Tempest* into Welsh in 2012. It was a technical challenge to keep the lines in metre because, not only does Welsh poetry count syllables, not accents, the basic unit of sound in Welsh is the mirror image of that in English. Shakespeare wrote in iambic pentameter (ti-TUM, ti-TUM, ti-TUM, ti-TUM, ti-TUM). In Welsh the accent of a word is, as a rule, on the penultimate syllable, giving one a trochaic rhythm (TUM-ti, TUM-ti, TUM-ti, TUM-ti, TUM-ti). I shouldn't have been too worried about these mirror images metrically: all I did was to steal an unaccented syllable from the end of the previous line to give an overall iambic rhythm. There was, however, one very interesting exception. I discovered that the songs in the play are composed in the Welsh trochaic measure. We know that Shakespeare included Welsh in his history plays because he had Welsh-speaking actors in his company. One of Shakespeare's grandmothers is said to have been a Welsh speaker, so I wonder if, in writing lyrics, closer to his linguistic subconscious, he was reproducing rhythms he'd heard very young at home.

Here's the concluding part of Ariel's first song sequence in the play, describing the magic shipwreck conjured up by Prospero, acting as a playwright. Note how this watery grave is a portrait of a father transformed by the sea and illusion into a piece of art. We're in Illyrian territory:

Full fathom five thy father lies,
Of his bones are coral made;
Those are pearls that were his eyes,
Nothing of him that doth fade
But doth suffer a sea-change
Into something rich and strange. (*ll.* 396-412) [23]

Yn y dyfnder mae dy dad
Cwrel yw ei esgyrn o
Dyna berl lle bu ei lygad,
Mae pob elfen sydd yn gwywo
Yn trawsnewid fel y môr
Nid trengi ond troi'n drysor. [24]

This is the watery, rhythmic place without which no art can be produced.

As you might expect with such an important place, this pre-linguistic, musical core, like Sean O'Brien's mere, is a contested space. For Seamus Heaney, it was the bog. Feminists in Ireland criticised Heaney's bog poems as for being sexist. No woman wants to be represented in a poem – even a great one! – as a dead sacrifice. In response, partly to this, Nuala Ní Dhomhnaill's poem 'Quicksand' makes the case for solid land:

Thíos ann tá giúis is bogdéil ársa;
tá cnámha na bhFiann 'na luí go sámh ann
a gclaimhte gan mheirg — is cailín báite,
rópa cnáibe ar a muineál tairrice.

Tá sé anois ina lag trá rabharta,
ta gealach lán is tráigh mhór ann
is anocht nuair a chaithfead mo shúile a dhúnadh
bíodh talamh slán, bíodh gaineamh chruaidh romham.

Down there there's ancient wood and bogdeal:
the Fianna's bones are there at rest
with rustless swords — and a drowned girl,
a noose around her neck.

Now there is a weak ebb-tide:
the moon is full, the sea will leave the land
and tonight when I close my eyes
let there be terra firma, let there be hard sand.[25]

The 'hard sand' for which Ní Dhomhnaill longs is more of a wish than a conviction. As any sailor knows, terra firma is dangerous. It's land, not the sea, that sinks your boat. The poet's fantasy leads her to a paradoxical place. Neaps, or 'weak ebb tides' can't happen at full moon, so even though Ní Dhomhnaill says she wants solid land, she's not going to get much of it. The position from which she's writing is uncanny and, for all the politics of gender, Ní Dhomhnaill is, as any poet would, responding to the watery, dangerous place without which she can't write.

Einstein's rejection of one sacrosanct 'time' or 'space' has implications for how we describe literary tradition and write poems. I'd like to pay attention here to the work of Anne Carson, who is one of the most radical interrogators of the contemporary lyric self. A Greek scholar, Carson edited an important edition of Sappho's work, reproducing the gaps in the text and making them part of the meaning. In a *Paris Review* interview Carson states that

there's something about Greek that seems to go deeper into words than any modern language. So that when you're reading it, you're down in the roots of where words work, whereas in English, we're at the top of the tree, in the branches, bouncing around. It was stunning to me, a revelation. And it continues to be stunning, continues to be like a harbor always welcoming. Strange, but welcoming.[26]

This statement started my anti-nationalistic antennae twitching, so I asked two friends who are classicists if they agreed with Carson's claim that Greek is closer to the nature of words than linguistic Johnny-come-latelies like English. No, they said. Plato and Aristotle have survived because they were clear thinkers, not because the Greek language gave them privileged access to reality. So much for that claim.

Carson's book *Nox*, which appeared in 2010, doesn't even look like a book. 'Box' would be a better description of the text. It is, simultaneously, an elegy to her brother, a translation of Catullus's poem 101 on the same theme and a meditation on the connections between history and grief. It straddles the genres of memoir, criticism and classical scholarship. The shape of the volume does the same thing. It's a mock scrapbook, constructed in a folding roll, with entries cut and pasted in (complete with stains and watermarks) and photographs. The surface of the page gives a cunning impression of layers. The verso of a page is implied, even though there's no there there. I checked, time and again, if there was text on the reverse and never quite believed that there wasn't. Here is opacity and transparency at the same time. The piece is like a film set, all front and illusion of depth. I'm a reader who marks passages of interest in pencil, and it's deeply pleasing to find that on these pages, my marks look as if they were intended by the author. Carson's collage engages us sufficiently to keep us reading but gives the reader ample room to think about his or her own family archive of letters and photographs. Some critics have attacked the book as presenting the apparatus of poetry without anything recognisable as a poem. Here we see lyricism fall into the abatement and low price described by Count Orsino and that, I think, for Carson, is the point.

Carson prepares her translation of the Catullus poem by taking us through each Latin word in the original by turn, although we only realise that she engaged in translating at the end of the work. She proposes the process of scholarship is itself a model for the retrieval of memory and emotion. Carson's glosses form the closest entities to 'traditional' poems in the book. For us non-classicists the status of Carson's gloss is difficult to gauge. Is it a quotation? Or the fruit of her own reading? Has she invented some of the examples and shades of meaning? I'd like to quote one entry in full:

vectus

veho vehere vexi vectum

[cf. Skt *vahati*, Gk ŏxos, OHG wagan, Eng wain] to convey from one place to another by bodily effort, to carry (a rider), to convey (of vehicles, ships, etc.), to carry (of draught animals); (of things, with diminished idea of motion) to sustain a load; to cause to be transported, bring; (of wind, water, etc.) to carry along, bear along; *in pericula vectus:* driven into danger; (of time) to carry with it, bring; to cause to extend or stretch from one point to another, to travel by some or other conveyance; to travel by sea, sail; to ride, drive; (poetical) to be carried on wings, fly; vecta spolia: borne in triumph; *per noctem in nihilo vehi:* to vanish by night into nothing; *quod fugiens semel hora vexit:* what the transient hour brought once and only once.

In some ways the status of this etymology doesn't matter. Carson is giving an account of the sea, which connects two destinations. In this, it's similar to metaphor. Both move things from one place to another by translation.

One of the discomfiting aspects of *Nox* is that the concertina shape and lack of page numbers makes navigating through the poem, if that's what it is, an unfamiliar experience. You look for one passage, fail to find it but discover another on the way. It's like going by dead reckoning in a landscape, as the GPS signal of pagination has gone down. On some pages, a single line is set into a deckled cut-out of the page as, for example, with 'It is for God to fix the time who knows no time.' Above this statement is what looks like part of a sea wall, with water beyond. The volume's unconventional form attacks the notion of sequence but its orderly progress through the Catullus poem, word by word, gives the sense of an alternative order being followed, rather than no form at all.

The sea is everywhere in this poem. Pages are marked by salt tears. A photograph of Carson's dead brother shows him as a young boy waving on a beach, the sea tranquil behind him. 'I love the old questions' reads the caption beneath. We learn that the brother's ashes are cast out to sea. Later on the poet says that her brother's 'death came wandering slowly towards me across the sea'. Underneath another caption appears from a lower layer of paper stating: 'Something inbetween, something so deeply swaying.' Overleaf is a collage of the same sea wall with what appears to be part of a boat's prow from another place It's like that magical shot in Herzog's *Nosferatu* of a pilot-less boat bringing the vampire's body into Germany. I think that the triumph of *Nox* is that, without setting out to do so literally, it's an exploration of the new human terrain, also explored by W.N. Herbert, of which the internet is the physical manifestation. Carson is giving an account of the sea that which connects two destinations, the space which makes metaphor possible. I'll be focusing on metaphor in my third lecture.

These same waters surround Shakespeare's final island in his last play, *The Tempest*, his most complete statement about the nature of his own art. This is a quantum sea, in which cause and effect bear a mysterious relationship to each other. These are the waters surrounding the island in *The Tempest*. As courtiers from Milan pick themselves up from being shipwrecked on the beach, the good old Gonzalo comments:

> Methinks our garments are now as fresh as when we put them
> on first in Africa, at the marriage of the King's fair daughter
> Claribel to the King of Tunis. (*ll.* 70-72)[27]

Those of you who go to sea will know how eye-wateringly bad
sailors smell when they come ashore. Imagine attending the
best wedding of your life – in a scorching climate – being at
sea, then shipwrecked and still smelling as fresh as a daisy!
Like this sea, poetry is a time-based form which uses its medium
to defy chronology. In Shakespeare's island plays, this operates
at both plot and lyric level. The music in *The Tempest* isn't in
the control of the human characters and can't be switched off
by them. Caliban is used to it and urges the clowns:

> Be not afeard. The isle is full of noises,
> Sounds and sweet airs that give delight and hurt not. (*ll.* 135-36)[28]

These aren't toxic melodies I discussed in my first lecture.
This, I suggest, is a symbolic description of the heart of Shake-
speare's poetry in himself. When Gonzalo the loyal courtier is
woken from the enchanted sleep into which Ariel has cast him,
he tells the others 'Upon mine honour, sir, I heard a humming,/
And that a strange one too, which did awake me.' (*ll.* 318-20)[29]
Here, I believe, Shakespeare is working back upstream to the
source of virtue and musicality to a hum. Poet and critic Angela
Leighton has written about the hum which Tennyson heard
behind modern life and which he equated often with distant
waters:

> Oh! pleasant breast of waters, quiet bay,
> Like to a quiet mind in the loud world,
> Where the chafed breakers of the outer sea
> Sank powerless.[30]

Here is a centre that behaves not according to Newtonian but
quantum physics. This is what poets listen to and where they
live.

This centreless centre is what makes art healthful. In *A Hos-
pital Odyssey*, I thought it was important to have a vision of

health, rather than to define everything by its opposite. Even further, I wanted to broaden the definition of health to include that difficult but fertile place I described in my first lecture. Just before they land on Hy-Brazil, Maris and her companions are moving through the hosts of the dead and are granted a vision of Helen of Troy. For me, she's not the seductress of popular myth but the embodiment of physical health manifested in supreme beauty. My Helen is fully immersed in the quantum sea:

> An underwater breeze
> made them shiver. Then a dynamic shimmer
> silvered the water. An electric charge
> thrilled through Ludlow, made Maris quiver.
> It was a feeling like spring fever,
>
> the excitement of making rough love.
> It was like the feeling of new-mown grass,
> a delirium. Maris felt herself alive
> like a comb of cells with surplus
> sweetness, dripping with rapturous
>
> honey. And suddenly the black
> was burnished, filled with a pulse
> which, to the ear of her ear, came back
> like the faintest music of sensuous dances,
> such as the wild extravagance
>
> that moves kelp forests with the hiss
> of everything tearing but then made whole
> by its own movement, which is bliss.
> Maris felt newly viable,
> vigorous, fresh and pliable
>
> as corn in a field, which you can hear grow
> on summer nights, if you care to listen.[31]

I'll be talking about form and particle physics, paying particular attention to metaphor and rhyme in my next lecture.

Quantum Poetics

Every poem is a cosmology. In my first lecture, I argued that, in order to write, poets have to enter a difficult emotional terrain that is, nevertheless, essential to their mental health. It's both glorious and dreadful but is an unpopular destination in general. My second lecture showed that this desert appears in another aspect, as a watery, rhythmic place which is still the pre-linguistic source of all art. I described this in terms of the sea, using it as an image for the quantum effects of surrendering to such a medium. I called it Illyria, after the island in Shakespeare's *Twelfth Night,* because that solid land is vibrating to the sea around it. In my final lecture, I'm going to consider poetic form in relation to quantum physics, suggesting that there's a deep congruence between the structure of the physical world and poetry itself. In fact, I'm going argue that, in certain ways, the world behaves like a poem and that poetry itself is a kind of science.

I'd like to start my discussion of poetic form by considering metaphor, which I think is more fundamental a device in poetry than either rhyme, metre, or alliterative patterning. Our eyes are made of meat and it's hard to see. Much of being human consists of simply trying to work out what is it exactly that I'm seeing out there? 'It is a bird? is it a plane? No, it's Superman!' From its earliest days, poetry's job has been to relate what's perceived as the exterior world to the body and to language. Hence, we have, in the Skaldic poetry of the Scandinavian Middle Ages, complex metaphorical puzzles. These translations show that stating one thing in terms of another is a basic social pleasure. Here are some lines from *The Kings' Sagas*:

Svalg hvert hús
heitum munni
viðar hundr
Verma bygðar
ok sviþkárr
selju rakki
of garðshlið
grenjandi fór.[1]

The literal translation of this verse reads:

The hound of the forest [FIRE] swallowed every house of the settlement of the Vermir with its hot mouth, and the violent dog of the willow [FIRE] ran howling through the yard-gate.[2]

Working this out is a game of ratios, a mathematical exercise. Fire is to wood as dog is to hunt. The poems are in code, so you need to be in the know. I have a Serbian friend who says that Soviet jokes are so alike in all Eastern European countries that citizens of Belgrade and Budapest can say to each other: 'Joke Number 3' and laugh uproariously at the same thing. A continuation of the gag has a citizen citing 'Number 6'. No reaction. 'You didn't tell it right.'

The kennings rely on a cluster of known meanings. The Anglo-Saxon riddles work quite differently. Here's one from the eleventh-century Exeter Book:

The wave, over the wave, a wierd [sic] thing I saw,
Thorough-wrought, and wonderfully ornate:
A wonder on the wave – water became bone.[3]

The author here wants the listener to fail at guessing the object being described, its metaphor is a booby trap. The "answer" is ice.

Returning to the kennings, I'm fascinated to notice that, for the Norse poet, the mouth was an image of the sea. In my second lecture last week, I showed how Shakespeare and other writers identified the sea with the pre-linguistic core of the creative imagination, the source of all rhythm and form. Listen to this:

Skaut vínfars
vísa mönnum
á gómsker
gyltu borði,
hilmis hirð
en hunangsbára
í geðknörr
glymjandi fell.[4]

The translation shows how intimately the warrior's body is related to the ocean:

The gilded rim of the wine-vessel [CUP] thrust against the gum-skerries [TEETH] of the leader's men, and the honey-wave [MEAD] fell foaming into the mind-ship [BREAST] of the ruler's retinue.[5]

The idea here is that the warrior's sternum is like the prow of a boat and that downing a good cup of mead is like shipping what sailors call 'a wet one.' It's clear from other verses that waves are explicitly linked to poetry. This is from a poem called 'Gold-Shortage':

Eisar vágr fyr (vísa
verk) rǫgnis mér (hagna),
þytr Óðrøris alda
(aldr) hafs við fles galdra.
              (Stanza 3)

The wave of Rǫgnir [ODIN, that is, POETRY] rushes before the prince. I always benefit from the works. The wave of the sea of Óðrørir [POETRY] roars against the rocks of chanting [TEETH].[6]

Unsurprisingly, perhaps, for such consummate seamen, the Norse knew where Illyria was. So, eight centuries before Jacques Maritain described the pulsions, or pre-artistic rhythms, fanning out from the subconscious, here are the Skalds using exactly the same imagery, suggesting that this is a mythic and universal aspect of how the internal and external landscape overlap.

One of the reasons that I like physicists so much is that they are just as concerned as poets are about what may accurately be said about the world. Physicists use words metaphorically in order to describe material phenomena. Particles, therefore, are metaphorical billiard balls, orreries, smudges, waves because that's the only way we can begin to imagine them. These images are constantly being revised in order to reach towards a better formulation of matter. The figurative "harmony of the spheres" has been updated in favour of spectra and wormholes.

The medieval Welsh *dyfalu* is a poetic technique that's akin to but more sophisticated than the Anglo-Saxon riddles. *Dyfalu* meant 'to compare' in the fifteenth century but, in the seventeenth, it came to mean 'to hypothesise'. So, just like an alchemist, a poet conducts metaphorical experiments in his or her work and holds theories about the nature of reality. Here's an example from the corpus of Taliesin, the poet I talked about earlier in relation to Dylan Thomas. One of his greatest odes begins by challenging the listener: 'Guess who it is.' The word used in Welsh – 'Dechymic' – has evolved into 'dychymyg', the imagination, so our name for the faculty still has this gaming, experimental overtone:

Dechymic pwy yw:	Guess who it is,
creat kyn Dilyw,	created before the Flood,
creadur kadarn	Strong creature
heb gic, heb ascwrn,	with no flesh or bone,
heb wytheu, heb waet,	no veins, no blood,
heb pen a heb traet.	no head and no feet.[7]

It is, of course, the wind.

Dafydd ap Gwilym's fourteenth-century poem on the same subject transforms the quasi-riddle into a virtuoso enactment of the wind's action. I consider ap Gwilym to be of a stature comparable to François Villon, a century later. The poem's so energetic that reading the whole thing leaves me out of breath. This is a riddle in reverse. We start with the answer and go out into wonder:

Yr wybrwynt, helynt hylaw,
Agwrdd drwst a gerdda draw,
Gŵr eres wyd garw ei sain,
Drud byd heb droed heb adain.
Uthr yw mor eres y'th roed
O bantri wybr heb untroed,
Yr awr hon dros y fron fry.[8]

Skywind, skillful disorder,
Strong tumult walking by there,
Wondrous man, rowdy-sounding,
Hero, with nor foot nor wing.
Yeast in cloud loaves, who's been thrown out
Of sky's pantry with not one foot
How swiftly you run, and so well
This moment above the high hill.[9]

The rapid change of terms, builds up into a virtuoso sequence and so, gives the impression of a world too hot for words to handle. I imagine the poet like a furniture remover trying to carry a piano downstairs. It's a big piece, awkward to manoeuvre around corners. If it falls, the man underneath will be injured.

With his interest in folk sayings, Paul Muldoon has caught this system of ratios exactly in a poem called 'Recalculating' from his collection *Songs and Sonnets*. Muldoon's first calculation is the overall count of syllables on his fingers – the basic arithmetic of metre, which used to be called 'numbers'. The second is Muldoon working out the ratios of a riddle but, as this is a Muldoon poem, it characteristically cuts us adrift from being able to find a solution:

Arthritis is to psoriasis as Portugal is to Brazil.
Brazil is to wood as war club is to war.
War is to wealth as performance is to appraisal.
Appraisal is to destiny as urn is to ear.[10]

In terms of rhyme, Brazil goes with appraisal and war goes with ear but, cutting it a different way, arthritis goes with Portugal and psoriasis with Brazil. By the last line, I'm beginning to suspect that Muldoon is being random. Having presented one set of relationships, the second section of the poem rejigs them:

> Wait. Isn't arthritis to psoriasis as Brazil is to Portugal?
> Portugal is to fado as Boaz is to Ruth.
> Ruth is to cornfield as wave is to particle.[11]

What particularly caught my interest here is in the line 'Ruth is to cornfield as wave is to particle.' Everybody knows that light can behave both as a particle and as a wave. Here's Brian Greene's elegant and informative formulation:

> the success of quantum mechanics forces us to accept that the electron, a constituent of matter that we normally envision as occupying a tiny, pointlike region of space, also has a description involving a wave that, to the contrary, is spread through the entire universe.[12]

This holds for all particles. So, 'Ruth' is the mythic name threading through the whole universe whereas the particular historical field in which she gathered tares is the particle. Or is it vice versa? By the end of the poem, all distinctions collapse because everything can be expressed in terms of everything else. The recalculation Muldoon is engaged in is one that produces its own small universe and then, pouff! it disappears.

When it comes to technical complexity, the medieval Welsh strict metres, called *cynghanedd*, has Anglo-Saxon alliteration knocked into a cocked hat. W.H. Auden used to recommend that young poets learn their craft by writing small three- and four-line *englynion*. (He also said to the bluestocking mother of a friend that no female intellectual should be seen without a typewriter.) I used to sneak off at break time in school to learn this way of writing from Mrs Eileen Beasley, a cultured and patriotic teacher in her office at the back of the Biology lab. If free verse is paddling in the sea, *cynghanedd* is kite surfing. Here's Dewi Wyn of Eifion's heroic vision of the Menai Suspension Bridge in a small stanza:

Uchelgaer uwch y weilgi – gyr y byd
  ch ´lg˘ | ch ´ lg | g r b´d

    Ei gerbydau drosti.
    g rb´ d˘

  Chwith<u>au</u>, holl long<u>au</u> y lli,
      <u>au</u> | ll / <u>au</u> | ll´

  Ewch o dan ei chadwyni.[13]
  ch   d´n | ch d´ n˘

High fort above salt water – drives the world
    From one side to the other.
Ships, boats and ocean liners,
Go under the chains that suspend her.[14]

I want to use *cynghanedd* to illustrate a principle which holds
for all poetry, even free verse. This system of euphony, *cyghanedd*,
appeared suddenly and unexpectedly in the fourteenth century.
It built on a loose patterning in early Welsh poetry by combining
it with French measures brought by the Normans to Britain.
Poets like Dafydd ap Gwilym multiplied the patterns available
to them by drawing on words from three languages – Welsh,
English and French. There are four main patterns of *cynghanedd*,
and any number of faults. Manuals are still being written about
the philosophy of the system. Such complexity was made
possible by the nature of Welsh itself, which has a system of
mutations. Apparently "solid" words alter in response to their
neighbours, thus multiplying the aural options available to the
poet. Each word in a sentence in Welsh can't decide how it
sounds until it's established its exact relationship to every
other. For example: *a* cat – cath, *the* cat, y gath. I can be *with*
a cat, â chath or, God forgive me, *in* a cat, yng nghath. Thus,
the word 'cat' exists in four guises. Words spark off each other
or rub up to and cuddle their fellow passengers in a sentence.
They have a quantum fuzziness at their edges, the sound they
make is purely relational. The theology of *cynghanedd* matches
the quantum entanglement described earlier in these lectures.
The ability to write under such handicaps served to distinguish
the educated court poets associated with the Welsh aristocrats

from folk versifiers. Such an intricate displacement activity must have had a political dimension. The last Prince of Wales was killed in 1282. For all the virtuosity of the technique, I feel an anxiety at its root, a sense that the world evades even our most ingenious formations.

This is verse that can earn a cross or a tick, according to whether it's technically correct or not. That's one of the reasons why I don't write in it now. I am a formalist but, as you'll see by the end of this lecture, I think that poetry's content is just as, if not more, important to me than its technical effects. *Cynghanedd* has moved with the times. It's used to rap and works well on Twitter It also fed into twentieth-century modernism through Gerard Manley Hopkins and Dylan Thomas. Its strictures embed the poet so firmly into the sonic materiality of language that it shows some of the quantum effects of the musicality behind language, the rhythms on which words are strung.

Let's look at an example of how Dafydd ap Gwilym uses this sonic indeterminacy to say more in his lines than should, strictly speaking, be possible. This extract is from a poem called 'Y Deildy' ('The House of Leaves'). I've marked up the pattern of corresponding consonants and accents:

Dewin fy nhŷ | a'i dawnha,
D   n   n ´ | d   n ´
Dwylo Mai | a'i hadeila,
D ´   l ˘ (m) | d ´ l ˘
A'i linyn yw'r gog | lonydd
    l ´n ˘   (r g g) | l ´ n ˘
A'i ysgwîr | yw eos gwŷdd,
    sg ´ | sg   ´
A'i dywydd | yw hirddydd | haf
            | h ´ | h ´
A'i ais | yw goglais | gwiwglaf,
        | g ´gl ˘ | g   ´   gl ˘
Ac allor serch | yw'r gelli
g   ´ll ˘(r s r ch | r) g ´ ll ˘
Yn gall, | a'i fwyall | wyf fi.[15]
        | f ´   ˘ | f ´

A magician renews my bower,
May's hands build it over,
The cuckoo's call's its measure
The nightingale its square,
Long summer days its weather,
Its walls made of love's shiver,
Woods' altar's love's obsession,
Its axe is me, made sane.[16]

The verbal patterning is so dense here that it's as if the poet is capturing an earlier version of our universe, one closer to the verbal Big Bang, when sounds and material – represented by rhyme and consonants – were packed closer together. This euphony is no add-on to Dafydd's work but *is* the poem's content. Phonically, poet, bird and tree are made of the same stuff and could change into each other at any moment. Here we have all the rural delights – birds, fine weather, sex – but, behind this complex description, somewhere in the distance we can hear a pulse: 'Dewin fy nhy a'i dawnha/ Dwylo Mai a'i hadeila.' It's barely registered but it's the poet measuring out the length of his lines, like pieces of wood and hewing them. Then, in the mind, we hear an answering pulse:

And then there was a pile of wood [...]
It was a cord of maple, cut and split
And piled – and measured, four by four by eight.
And not another like it could I see.
No runner tracks in this year's snow looped near it.[17]

Dafydd conceives of his work as woodcraft, and his own mind as an axe: 'Its axe is me, made sane.' The same axe crops up in another poem in a new world:

                    I thought that only
Someone who lived in turning to fresh tasks
Could so forget his handiwork on which
He spent himself, the labor of his ax,
And leave it there far from a useful fireplace
To warm the frozen swamp as best it could
With the slow smokeless burning of decay.[18]

49

Robert Frost's 'The Wood-Pile', February 1912. Both poets, through us readers, are standing, each in his forest, straining to hear the sound of the other at his work. This is the place – being desert, sea or woodland – for which poets listen and where strange things happen to them and to time. Literary lineages work backwards as well as forwards.

Einstein argued that backward-causation couldn't take place and is usually this is true. Think of time's arrow, which means that you don't hear my words until I've spoken them. However, there is a ghostly action of the future on the past which acts on an experiment. That is, at a certain point of a comparison, an exchange occurs between past and present. Therefore, if we consider each metaphor and, by extension, each poem, as an experiment, then the normal rules of causality are suspended for the duration of the trial.[19]

In a letter to Henry Treece on 23 March 1938, Dylan Thomas describes this phenomenon exactly in relation to his work:

> a poem of mine is, or should be, a watertight section of the stream that is flowing all ways; all warring images within it should be reconciled for that small stop of time.[20]

If every poem is a cosmology, then each metaphor is an attempt at a Grand Theory of Everything. As MRI scans show, metaphorical thinking involves both sides of the brain simultaneously and this may be part of its pleasure. The congruence between the physical laws of the universe and our brains' ability to perceive it makes me wonder if metaphor isn't an universal structural principle of matter. If everything is related to everything else, then metaphor changes from being a 'fanciful' symbol into a form of scientific experiment. In Fritjof Capra's words:

> Quantum theory forces us to see the universe not as a collection of physical objects but rather as a complicated web of relations between the various parts of the unified whole.[21]

All poetry's techniques boil down to this 'complicated web of relations' between 'the various parts of the unified whole.'

I've noticed something very interesting in relation to time and metaphor. I mentioned the idea of time's arrow just now. Briefly stated, it's the concept that physical processes have an inbuilt direction, that is, from order to disorder. The egg, which was snug in its cardboard box, falls and shatters into many pieces, with a splat of yolk. Smashed eggs tend not to lift themselves off the floor, gather themselves together and put themselves back neatly in the egg box. This principle is built into the universe because, with the Big Bang, matter started in a simplified state and the laws of probability mean that it moves in the direction of entropy, that is, increased chaos.[22] If you say that a mattress is as bloody as a butcher's apron, it also makes sense to say that a butcher's apron can be as bloody as a mattress.[23] In George Herbert's 'Constancie', he portrays the honest man as one who

> when the day is done,
> His goodnesse sets not, but in dark can runne:
> The sunne to others writeth laws,
> And is their vertue; Vertue is his Sunne.[24]

The sun is virtue, virtue is the sun, even at night. The metaphor is a reversible coat, it can be worn one way then turned inside out. In these cases metaphor's arrow points both ways. Humpty Dumpty can fall and put himself back together again.

However, this isn't always the case. Let's take a very famous example from Philip Larkin's 'Aubade', a poem about the fear of death, describing dawn coming to a street, watched by a sleepless man. The final line reads: 'Postmen like doctors go from house to house.'[25] This speaker is foreseeing his own death in hospital, which is why he perceives postmen as doctors, dosing each door with the medicine of mail. Try it in reverse, though, and it doesn't work: 'Doctors like postmen go from bed to bed.' In this case, the arrow of metaphor can't be reversed. What's lost is the precise action of forcing medicine through a stiff letterbox. In hospital, it's nurses, not doctors who administer medicine to patients, so the postman needs to be a woman to make the comparison match perfectly. 'Postmen like nurses go from house to house' is metrically identical to Larkin's line and is more life-like. Larkin decided he wanted the extra authority of the doctor figure, in order to increase the terror of the image.

Rhyme is metaphor's aural equivalent. It posits an euphonic connection between words and, by extension, suggests a substantial relationship between different objects to which they refer. Children's delight in rhyme suggests that it's fundamental to language acquisition. Rhyme, in itself, encourages metaphor. For example, from the *Rhyming Dictionary*, I take, at random, the words 'zebra' and 'cause célèbre'. My rhyme is ready-made. In order to connect the two nouns, I have to create a relationship that makes sense. I draw an analogy between the black lines on a zebra's hide and the newsprint generated by a scandal. I imagine zebras trampling a zoo-keeper to death and, soon we're seeing through a two-way mirror: the zebra pattern on the front page of the *New York Times* and a newspaper story on the flanks of a herd of zebras ignoring the fading cries of the naturalist under their hooves.

I decided to rhyme *A Hospital Odyssey*, my epic poem because I felt that form would give me stamina over a distance. I rhymed some five and a half thousand lines, a b a b b, in a measure that I adapted from the ballades of François Villon. This was a kind of experiment in itself. When I use rhyme, I'm composing my stanza both backwards from my rhyme word and forward at the pace of narrative sense. While I'm working, therefore, my mind is, as Dylan Thomas discussed, 'flowing all ways'. This movement backwards and forwards along the one line happens at two different speeds. As I was writing, I'd often have rhyme schemes mapped out a few stanzas in advance, without any idea of how I was going to hit a certain mark by the end of a speech. The musical structure of the poem existed in my subconscious before the narrative.

Rhyme limits the words you can use at the end of a line by pushing you towards a certain musical way of saying something.

This choice becomes statistical and political at the same instant. Just because it's easy to rhyme certain words in a language, doesn't mean that you should accept the easy options. For example, 'womb' is an old rhyme with 'tomb,' the poet's aural memory hears it straight away. I might want to resist the old identification of the female with death for political reasons because I reject that concept.

In physics, Heisenberg's Uncertainty Principle dismissed the idea of the measurable world being solidly "out there". It shows that you can't know a particle's position and its momentum at the same time, so that its location can only be described in terms of probability. I find a direct analogy between this and the way I play rhyme's flow both with and against cliché. I see writing in rhyme as an enactment of the laws of physics. When I approach the end of a line, the language offers me a certain number of rhymes, all of which are equally likely to work so, I hear them all simultaneously. This is the closest I ever get to seeing Illyria. The moment I choose one word, this vista collapses and I lose that field of potential sound which I glimpsed for one moment.

Every poem is a possible world. I had tutorials in particle physics to enable me to write the part of *A Hospital Odyssey* that takes place in outer space. One afternoon, with the help of Professor Mike Edmunds of the Cardiff School of Physics and Astronomy, I even calculated the size of the universe with my 'O'-level Maths. In this section of the poem, Hardy, Maris's husband, is experiencing a crisis during a stem-cell transplant:

Maybe not then, but this is what Hardy saw
from his dying: Maris, bending over him
and, behind her the vibrant, dazzling core
of the sun, rich and red as haemachrome
at fifteen million degrees. He was overcome

by the knowledge that everything 'out there'
was, in truth, his own body. We're filaments
of light, we're talking with everywhere
at once, and we were never meant
to be thought of as single, lines to be bent

in the space-time continuum.
That's prose. No, it's more like the drive
of poetry. It's as when I rhyme,
there's always a nano-second before I've
chosen a word when I perceive

all its homophones at once
before the end-word's probability wave
collapses, before I take a chance
on one meaning, when my mind revolves
with the quantum mechanics that makes stars evolve

from the tiniest jitters. We're born
to catastrophe. Galaxies fly
away from each other in identical forms.
Matter never sees fit to die
and if life is the transfer of energy

from one state to another – this poem from me
to you – then this continual exchange
must be our purpose. Infinity's
birdsong continues just beyond the range
of our human hearing. Love is the hinge

on which it all turns.[26]

I've talked a good deal about poetic form in this lecture, but
I want to conclude by arguing for content. It's all very well to
appreciate the poetic technique of poetry but this is only half
the story. It's like describing light only as waves, when we know
that it's also particles. Wallace Stevens argued that poetry isn't
an aesthetic activity separate from reality, it is the universe and
is, therefore, factual:

> The imagination never brings anything into the world but, on the
> contrary, like the personality of the poet in the act of creating,
> it is no more than a process, and desiring with all the power of
> our desire not to write falsely, do we not begin to think of the
> possibility that poetry is only reality, after all, and that poetic
> truth is a factual truth, seen, it may be, by those whose range
> in the perception of fact – that is, whose sensibility – is greater
> than our own? [27]

Stevens's hyper-aestheticism, philosophising and metaphorical difficulty is, therefore, a form of realism. Quantum physics is no more than the mathematical expression of exactly the same world. Both equations and poems are judged according to their elegance and accuracy. Poetry models possible worlds. Nils Bohr contended that there is 'no quantum world. There is only abstract quantum description.' It makes no sense to talk about poetry apart from reality because the poem itself *is* the world.

David Bohm, took this even further, arguing that our mental processes are implicated in the whole. The important point here, I think, is that both writing and reading poetry are performative:

> So in a way, thought becomes a symbol or metaphor – an activity which is a living example of what infinite means, for when a thing truly displays its own inner nature, it is a microcosm of infinity. And isn't that what a good work of art is?
> […] At that moment, there is an *enactment of wholeness.*[28]

Some of Bohm's followers have extended his ideas as explanations for mystical phenomena. I'm suspicious of popular science which makes particle physics a new religion but, if physics is telling us that reality works in a way analogous to art, then it would explain why poetry is, objectively, such a fertile way of describing it.

Heinrich Herz described his predecessor James Clerk Maxwell's equations in terms which I apply to my own private collection of great poems by others. Maxwell himself wrote poetry, but I suspect his real aesthetic achievement lay in his science. Our understanding of electro-magnetic fields and much else is based on his equations, about which Herz, a man not given to extravagant praise, wrote:

> One cannot escape the feeling that these mathematical formulae have an independent existence and an intelligence of their own, that they are wiser than we are, wiser even than their discoverers, that we get more out of them than was originally put into them.[29]

The best poems do exactly this: they draw on the time and

experience of past poets (and future ones) to achieve effects which are beyond the reach of any individual writer. They defy logic, like the elusive process of cold fusion.

I want to thank you for accompanying me on these lectures' journey through creative despair, over the seas and into the forest of the subconscious. So, where do poets live? Somewhere and everywhere. Hugo of Saint Victor wrote about exile:

> It is, therefore, a great source of virtue for the practised mind to learn, bit by bit, first to change about in visible and transitory things, so that afterwards it may be able to leave them behind altogether. The man who finds his homeland sweet is still a tender beginner; he to whom every soil is as his native one is already strong; but he is perfect to whom the entire world is as a foreign land.[30]

Perhaps I should add here: as a quantum land.

NOTES

FIRST LECTURE
The Stronger Life

1. Gwyneth Lewis, *Sunbathing in the Rain: A Cheerful Book about Depression* (London: Harper Perennial, 2011), pp. 56-67.

2. ibid, pp. 50-52.

3. Kay Redfield Jamison, *Touched with Fire: Manic-Depressive Illness and the Artistic Temperament* (Riverside, NJ: Free Press, 1994).

4. Charlotte Waddell, 'Creativity and Mental Illness: Is there a Link?,' *Canadian Journal of Psychiatry*, March 1998, Vol 43, pp. 166-72.

5. Regina Derieva, *The Sum Total of Violations*, tr. Daniel Weissbort (Todmorden: Arc, 2009), p. 31.

6. Marion Milner (Joanna Field), *On Not Being Able to Paint* (Oxford, 1957), pp. 90-91.

7. Andrew Lycett, *Dylan Thomas: A New Life* (London: Weidenfeld, 2003), p. 374.

8. Elizabeth Bishop, *One Art: Letters*, selected and edited by Robert Giroux (London: Pimlico, 1994), pp. 276-77.

9. Elizabeth Bishop, ibid, p. 277.

10. ibid.

11. ibid, p. 281.

12. Eileen Simpson, *Poets in their Youth: A Memoir* (Faber: London, 1982), p. 253.

13. W.B. Yeats, *Selected Criticism*, ed. A. Norman Jeffares (London: Pan Books, 1976), p. 265.

14. Wallace Stevens, *The Necessary Angel: Essays on Reality and the Imagination* (Knopf: New York, 1951), pp. 153-54.

15. John Berryman, *Collected Poems: 1937-1971*, ed. Charles Thornbury (Faber: London, 1990), p. 221.

16. François Villon, *Selected Poems*, tr. Peter Dale (Harmondsworth: Penguin, 1978), p. 66.

17. Gwyneth Lewis, *A Hospital Odyssey* (Bloodaxe Books: Tarset, 2010), pp. 59-60 .

18. Laura Riding Jackson, *The Poems of Laura Riding: A New Edition of the 1938 Collection* (Manchester: Carcanet, 1980), p. 184.

19. Dylan Thomas, *Collected Poems: 1934-1953*, ed. Walford Davies & Ralph Maud (Dent: London, 1988), p. 262.

20. Dylan Thomas, *Early Prose Writings*, ed Walford Davies (London, 1971), p. 156.

21. Dylan Thomas, *Collected Poems*, p. 74.

22. For another translation of the same passage, see Hans-Georg Moeller, *Daoism Explained: From the Dream of the Butterfly to the Fishnet Allegory* (Open Court: New York, 2004), p 62.

SECOND LECTURE
What Country, Friends, is This?

1. William Shakespeare, *Twelfth Night or What You Will* (The Arden Shakespeare, third series), ed. Keir Elam (Arden Shakespeare: London, 2013), pp. 165-66, I, ii.

2. ibid.

3. William Shakespeare, *Twelfth Night* (The Arden Shakespeare), ed. J.M. Lothian & T.W. Craik (Methuen: London, 1975), Appendix 1, pp. 163-64.

4. See Brian Greene, *The Fabric of the Cosmos: Space, Time, and the Texture of Reality* (Penguin/Allen Lane: London, 2004), p. 80.

5. *The Holographic Paradigm and Other Paradoxes*, ed. Ken Wilber (Shambala: Boulder, CO, 1982), p. 1.

6. ibid, p. 21.

7. ibid, p. 62.

8. *A Hospital Odyssey*, pp. 125-26.

9. Orhan Pamuk, *Istanbul: Memories of a City*, tr. Maureen Freely (Faber: London, 2005), p. 232.

10. Matthew Hollis, *Now All Roads Lead to France: the Last Years of Edward Thomas* (Faber: London, 2011).

11. Quoted in R. George Thomas, *Edward Thomas: A Portrait* (Oxford, 1985), p. 80.

12. www.zamynfoundation.org/texts/ai-weiwei

13. Nuala Ní Dhomhnaill, *The Fifty Minute Mermaid*, tr. Paul Muldoon (Loughcrew, Oldcastle. Co. Meath: Gallery Press, 2007), pp. 150-51.

14. ibid, p 29.

15. Jacques Maritain, *Creative Intuition in Art and Poetry: The A.W. Mellon Lectures in the Fine Arts* (Princeton: Princeton University Press, 1953), p. 205.

16. ibid, p. 57.

17. ibid, p. 73.

18. Sean O'Brien, *The Drowned Book* (Picador: London, 2007), p. 18.

19. Thomas Hardy, *Satires of Circumstance: Lyrics and Reveries with Miscellaneous Pieces* (Macmillan: London, 1919), p 109

20. R.S. Thomas, *Collected Poems: 1945-1990* (Dent: London, 1993), p. 250.

21. W.N. Herbert, *Omnesia: Alternative Text* (Bloodaxe Books: Tarset, 2013), p. 21.

22. ibid, p. 40.

23. William Shakespeare, *The Tempest* (The Arden Shakespeare), ed. Virginia Mason Vaughan & Alden T. Vaughan (Bloomsbury: London, 1999), p 178, 1.2.

24. William Shakespeare, addasiad Gwyneth Lewis, *Y Storm* (Barddas, 2012), p. 27.

25. Nuala Ní Dhomhnaill, *Selected Poems/Rogha Dánta*, tr. Michael Hartnett (Dublin: Raven Arts, 1988), pp. 84-85.

26. Anne Carson, *The Paris Review*, The Art of Poetry No. 88 http://www.theparisreview.org/interviews/5420/the-art-of-poetry-no-88-anne-carson

27. *The Tempest*, p. 189, 2.1.

28. ibid, p. 232, 3.3.

29. ibid, p. 206, 2.2.

30. Alfred Lord Tennyson, 'The Lover's Tale', quoted in Angela Leighton, 'Tennyson's Hum', *The Tennyson Research Bulletin*, Vol. 9, No 4, November 2010, p. 318.

31. *A Hospital Odyssey*, p. 118.

THIRD LECTURE
Quantum Poetics

1. *Poetry from The Kings' Sagas 2: From c. 1035 to c. 1300*, ed. Kari Ellen Gade et al, p. 705.

2. ibid.

3. *Old English Riddles from the Exeter Book*, 2nd edition, tr Michael Alexander (Anvil Press: London, 1984), p 52.

4. *Poetry from the Kings' Sagas 2*, p. 721.

5. Sturla Þórðarson, 'Hákonarkviða', Skaldic Project Academic Body, University of Aberdeen, ed. Kari Ellen Gade.

6. 'From 'Vellekl', in *Poetry from the Kings' Sagas 1: From Mythical Times to c. 1035*, ed. Diana Whaley (Turnhout, Belgium: Brepols, 2013).

7. *Legendary Poems from the Book of Taliesin*, ed. & tr. Marged Haycock (Aberystwyth: CMCS Publications, 2007), p. 332.

8. *Cerddi Dafydd ap Gwilym*, gol Dafydd Johnson et al (Cardiff, 2010), p. 194.

9. tr. Gwyneth Lewis.

10. Paul Muldoon, *Songs and Sonnets* (Enitharmon: London, 2012), p. 41.

11. ibid.

12. Brian Greene, *op. cit.*, p. 90.

13. For a biography of Dewi Wyn o Eifion, see http://wbo.llgc.org.uk/en/s-OWEN-DAV-1784.html

14. tr. Gwyneth Lewis.

15. Cerddi Dafydd ap Gwilym, p. 164.

16. tr. Gwyneth Lewis.

17. *The Poetry of Robert Frost*, ed. Edward Connery Lathem (New York: Holt, Rinehart, and Winston, 1975), p. 101.

18. ibid, p.102.

19. See Paul Davies, *About Time: Einstein's Unfinished Revolution* (London: Penguin, 1995), p. 177.

20. Dylan Thomas, *The Collected Letters*, 2nd edition, ed. Paul Ferris (Dent: London, 2000), p. 329.

21. *The Holographic Paradigm*, p. 165.

22. See Brian Greene, op. cit, p. 175.

23. I owe this image to a conversation with Craig Raine.

24. *The English Poems of George Herbert*, ed. Helen Wilcox (Cambridge: Cambridge University Press, 2011), p. 263.

25. Philip Larkin, *Collected Poems*, ed. Anthony Thwaite (London: Faber, 1988), p. 208.

26. *A Hospital Odyssey*, pp. 145-46.

27. Wallace Stevens, *The Necessary Angel*, p. 59.

28. *The Holographic Paradigm*, p. 204.

29. Quoted by Prof Frank Wilczek, *Quantum Beauty*, Darwin College Lecture Series 2011, http://www.sms.cam.ac.uk/media/1096119.

30. Quoted in Edward W. Said, *The World, The Text, and the Critic* (Harvard University Press: Cambridge, MA, 1983), p. 7.